SOUTHERN REGION LOCOMOTIVES IN THE 1970s AND 1980s

Andy Gibbs

amberley

First published 2026

Amberley Publishing
The Hill, Stroud
Gloucestershire, GL5 4EP

www.amberley-books.com

Copyright © Andy Gibbs, 2026

The right of Andy Gibbs to be identified as the Author of this work has been asserted in accordance with the Copyrights, Designs and Patents Act 1988.

ISBN 978 1 3981 2493 6 (print)
ISBN 978 1 3981 2494 3 (ebook)

All rights reserved. No part of this book may be reprinted or reproduced or utilised in any form or by any electronic, mechanical or other means, now known or hereafter invented, including photocopying and recording, or in any information storage or retrieval system, without the permission in writing from the Publishers.

British Library Cataloguing in Publication Data.
A catalogue record for this book is available from the British Library.

Origination by Amberley Publishing.
Printed in the UK.

Appointed GPSR EU Representative: Easy Access System Europe Oü, 16879218
Address: Mustamäe tee 50, 10621, Tallinn, Estonia
Contact Details: gpsr.requests@easproject.com, +358 40 500 3575

Introduction

Welcome to this, my ninth book for Amberley Publishing. This sees me revert to type as a former British Rail Southern Region employee and indulge in all things Southern. Well, the locomotives at least! The two main Southern Region locomotive classes, 33 and 73, are covered photographically in depth. There are photos of every single member apart from those withdrawn very early due to accident damage. There are also images of Classes 07 and 09, the Southern's own high-speed shunter. Classes 70, 71 and 74 are also covered.

The Class 33 'Cromptons' and the Class 73 'ED's' were well thought out designs, and the Class 73s especially have lasted a very long time. Both locomotive types were built for mixed traffic applications, freight, parcels and passenger workings. The Class 33s were unique in being built from day one with electric train heating (ETH) and this versatility saw them eventually take over secondary passengers services over huge swathes of southern and western England, plus Wales and the north-west. Sadly those days are over, but in addition to the preserved examples there are still a handful running on the mainline.

The Class 73s have faired even better with many examples working for GB Railfreight and Network Rail. Further upgrades saw the class reaching the far north of Scotland working for Caledonian Sleeper.

Most images are scanned from 35-mm transparencies and black and white negatives, with some medium format transparencies and negatives.

I hope the photographs will bring back good memories of times that cannot be repeated and there are some very odd ones too. In a pre-digital age every photograph had to be considered before being taken – it cost money and a 36-exposure slide film was not cheap.

As always a big thanks to all the photographers who recorded a time that will not be repeated. Where known, photographers are credited in the book. Thanks also to the various 'gen' websites that have helped fill gaps in the image information, such as BR Loco database, RailGenArchive, Blood and Custard, Six Bells Junction and Class 33 Cromptons to name just a few. Thanks also to my former colleague John 'JKA' Atkinson for some help with train details and the members of RMweb, whose depth of knowledge is immeasurable.

I finish the book once again with a bottle of beer, this time a beer that has moved home from Partridge Green to Fuller's Brewery in London, Darkstar Hophead, a very nice former Sussex beer that I can now easily get in York.

Andy Gibbs

The Ruston & Hornsby Class 07s were introduced during 1962 to replace the remaining steam locomotives on the Southampton Docks network. Fourteen were built and here we find No. 07001 (formerly D2985) shunting 35-ton Class A tank wagons at Eastleigh. The class was an early victim to changes in traffic and a declining market. All bar one were withdran by 1977. Seven still exist, including this one, which after moving to Staveley Lime Works at Buxton became part of the Harry Needle fleet based at Barrow Hill. February 1975.

The driver of No. 07005 (formerly D2989) looks back down his train at Eastleigh. This locomotive was withdrawn in July 1977 and sold for further use at ICI Wilton. It is currently preserved on the Great Central Railway, Loughborough. February 1975.

No. D2995 (07011) is found deep in Southampton Docks doing what they were built for. In the background is the J. Rank Solent Flour Mill. Another Class 07 can be seen peeping out from behind a long line of Conflats and containers, c. 1966.

Captured between buildings at Eastleigh works No. 07011 (formerly D2995) shunts some wagons, the first containing scrapped wheelsets. A variety of Conflat and other wagons in the background the first siding loaded with containers. Ironically the massive increase in using 20- and 40-foot shipping containers was one of the reasons for this classes demise. No. 07011 lives on and is preserved at St Leonard's depot. February 1975.

New to Eastleigh depot in 1959 and after stints at most southern depots No. 09001 (D3665) didn't stray very far until privatisation. It and many of the Class 09s were then spread far and wide. Here at Allied Steel and Wire in Cardiff we find No. 09001. 12 June 1996.

The Class 09 originally consisted of twenty-six examples. They are a higher geared version of the Class 08 and have a maximum speed of 27 mph. Although initially allocated in the Midlands and North of England they all graduated to the Southern Region where they were fitted with high-level pipes for shunting EMU and DEMU vehicles. At Clapham Junction we find No. 09003 (formerly D3667) shunting a Southern Region-allocated Mk1 GUV. 1 November 1977.

It's a dreary wet day in Brighton as an ex-works No. 09004 (formerly D3668) brings the ECS for the Intercity service to Manchester Piccadilly into the station. There was a weekly overnight changeover of these locomotives with one being sent to Selhurst and the crew returning with a replacement. The trip took an age and wasn't popular with the traincrew. 14 July 1983.

No. 09007 (formerly D3671) shunts a Southern Region-allocated Mk1 BG, which is stencilled 'NOT in Common Use SR Southwestern Division only'. August 1980.

Stabled alongside Brighton Upper Goods signal box is No. 09012 (formerly D4100). New to the SR in 1961 and initially allocated to Ashford. An Opel Commodore can be glimpsed behind the signal box.

Deep inside Selhurst depot we find 09015 (formerly D4103) amongst a lot of wheelsets. This loco was also new to the SR in 1961, being allocated close by at Norwood. 21 September 1980.

At Bournemouth we find No. 09024 (formerly D4112), which was initially allocated to Nuneaton in 1961. After being allocated to various depots, including Rugby, Crewe, Allerton and Bristol Bath Road, it was transferred to the Southern Region in January 1976. 29 May 1979.

The Class 33s consisted of ninety-eight locomotives designed specifically for the Southern Region by the Birmingham Railway Carriage and Wagon Works (BRCW). Introduced from 1960, they were a more powerful development of Classes 26 and 27, also built by BRCW. At Dawlish Warren we find Nos 33001 (D6500) and 33023 (D6541) heading east with an unidentified service. 9 September 1979.

At Clapham Junction is No. 33001 with brake van, translator coach and a pair of Class 508 units. The Class 508s are being sent off to Liverpool for service on the Merseyrail network. The Southern will be getting Class 455s as replacement. One of the trailer vehicles from the Class 508s were used in the Class 455/7 fleet. 26 May 1984.

At Millbrook, to the west of Southampton, Nos 33002 (D6501) and 33040 (D6558) double-head 1V10, the 09.13 SO Brighton to Penzance service. The coaching stock unusually has three Mk2 FK coaches in the formation. No. 33002 was named *Sea King* in 1991. 18 July 1986.

Southern Region Locomotives in the 1970s and 1980s

No. D6502 was an early withdrawal, written off in March 1964 after being involved in a major collision at Itchingfield Junction, West Sussex. Earlier in its career we find it powering through Paddock Wood with a Folkestone to Charing Cross service. August 1960.

No. 33003 (D6503) is in charge of an engineers' train at Staines. The Grampus wagons are full to the brim with new wooden sleepers. The line to Windsor and Eton Riverside bears to the right, whilst the train is taking the route towards Virginia Water. 12 August 1976.

Strong winter sun illuminates No. 33004 (D6504) as it runs light engine through a snow-covered Redbridge. 9 January 1985. (P. Barber)

No. D6505 (later 33005) with its mix of Mk1 and Bulleid coaches in tow brakes for the curve at Tonbridge whilst working a Ramsgate to Cannon Street service. June 1960.

Curving into Salisbury, No. 33005 (D6505) is working 1V61, the 09.20 SO Brighton to Exeter St Davids. This train was double headed in the summer months, but a single Crompton would suffice during the winter. 7 February 1981. (J. Vaughan)

No. 33006 (D6506) storms past well-tended allotments at Elm Grove, Durrington, whilst working 1O85, the 15.10 Cardiff Central to Brighton. 26 April 1988. (J. Vaughan)

Pausing at Eastleigh is No. 33007 (D6507) with a long train of Presflo cement wagons, probably from Bevois Park sidings. June 1984.

The Reading to Tonbridge line via Redhill was the mainstay of the 3R 'Tadpole' DEMUs for many years. They were augmented in peak times by a few three-car Mk1 sets powered by a Class 33. We find such a train at Crowthorne with No. 33007 providing the power on 2O38, the 17.08 Reading to Redhill. September 1974.

At Dr Day's Junction near Bristol No. 33008 (D6508) powers along with 1V22, the 08.30 Brighton to Cardiff Central service. No. 33008 was named *Eastleigh* on 11 April 1980. 30 May 1984.

Sweeping round Bradford West Junction No. 33009 (D6509) makes a fine sight whilst working 1V46, the 08.30 Brighton to Cardiff Central service. It was named *Walrus* in 1991. 2 April 1988. (J. Vaughan)

A fine but cloudy day greets No. 33010 (D6510) as it approaches Reading with 1E12, the 14.14 Portsmouth Harbour to York Intercity cross-country service. 9 April 1985.

Swindon Works is the location for No. 33011 (D6512). During this period they were frequent visitors, bringing Class 411 4CEP EMUs to Swindon for refurbishment and taking completed units back to the Southern Region. November 1981.

Pottering eastbound through the centre road at Dawlish Warren, No. 33011 makes light work of a couple of German ferry vans and an ECC PBA china clay wagon. 12 August 1987.

At the north end of Eastleigh station, No. 33012 (D6515) pauses with a freight train. The first consists of a former SPA wagon, probably being used as a barrier wagon. 3 July 1979.

A busy scene at Kensington Olympia as No. 33013 (D6518) trundles southbound across the scissors crossing with the Chipmans weedkilling train. Northbound in the platform, No. 33008 waits to depart with a Class 302 EMU returning from Eastleigh works to Ilford. 11 August 1982.

A crisp winter's day in the Sussex countryside finds No. 33013 heading south with a short engineers' train, which includes a crane. In the distance road traffic crosses Adversane level crossing whilst a London-bound EMU heads towards Billingshurst. 10 December 1988. (J. Vaughan)

With a collection of BR and former LMS and SR parcels vans, No. 33014 (D6522) approaches Fareham station from Eastleigh. 21 April 1981.

At the eastern end of Southampton tunnel No. 33015 (D6523) bursts into the daylight with an unidentified Bristol to Portsmouth Harbour working. Class 33s were synonymous with this route until Sprinters took over the workings in the late 1980s. July 1986.

No. 33016 (D6524) is captured near Fleet with an unidentified pair of 4SUB units en route to the scrap man.

A nice and clean No. 33017 (D6526) crawls into the carriage sidings at Clapham Junction with an ECS move from Waterloo. An unidentified Class 33 brings up the rear. The platforms look deserted. 6 March 1984.

No. 33018 (D6530) starts to accelerate its train of former ESSO 45-ton tank wagons away from Reading station. 30 December 1983.

At Lewes No. 33019 (D6534) and an unidentified sister loco curve the line from Keymer Junction, passing Lewes signal box en route from Tolworth to Newhaven. These wagons were used to transport marine dredged shingle. The locomotive was named *Griffon* in 1991.

GO says the headcode and Nos 33019 and 33001 are going some with this Freightliner train at Sonning in Berkshire. 31 October 1980.

One service synonymous with the Cromptons was the Saturdays-only Brighton to Exeter St Davids train. Double-headed in the summer months with eleven or twelve coaches and eight coaches and just a single locomotive during the winter. At a wet Salisbury we find Nos 33019 and 33064 working 1O86, the 13.40 from Exeter back to Brighton. 15 August 1979. (J. Vaughan)

At Dundas near Bath we find No. 33020 (D6537) heading east with a well-loaded 1O96, the 15.10 Cardiff Central to Brighton. 23 April 1988. (G. Roose)

Under grey skies at Leamington Spa, No. 33021 (D6539) leads a train of containers heading south, bound for Southampton Docks. 10 September 1983.

Approaching Ludlow station is No. 33022 (D6540) working south with 1V02, the 08.01 Crewe to Cardiff Central service. 15 August 1981.

Under the overall roof at Manchester Piccadilly No. 33023 (D6541) has recently arrived with 1M70, the 07.50 from Swansea. The loco will return to South Wales on 1V05, the 13.45 departure to Cardiff Central.

Approaching Crowley Bridge just north of Exeter is No. D6542 (later 33024) with a service from Barnstaple. 17 July 1972.

At Blackwater on the Reading to Guilford line No. 33024 (D6542) is captured working the 17.08 Reading to Redhill service. The train is formed of a Mk1 Open Second, Brake Second and a GUV. This was one of a very small number of booked loco-hauled workings over this route. September 1974.

No. 33025 (D6543) *Sultan* waits to depart Bristol Temple Meads with an unidentified service to Portsmouth Harbour. The locomotive was named *Sultan* on 8 August 1981 after HMS *Sultan*, the Royal Navy's marine engineering school. August 1986.

On Dainton Bank in Devon we find No. D6544 (later 33026) with the Plymouth Friary to Fawley empty tanker train. Dainton Bank is one of the steepest gradients on the mainline railway ranging from 1 in 36 to 1 in 57. Even with the tankers empty the Crompton will be working hard. The locomotive was named *Seafire* in 1991. 10 April 1973.

In bright sunshine at Leamington Spa No. 33026 waits to depart with 1E22, the 12.46 Portsmouth Harbour to Leeds cross-country service. The Crompton worked the train as far as Birmingham New Street where No. 45143 took the train forward. 3 May 1985.

Southern Region Locomotives in the 1970s and 1980s

27

Exeter St Davids and a freshly painted No. 33027 (D6545) waits to depart with a train for London Waterloo as an unidentified Class 50 arrives from the west. No. 33027 was later named *Earl Mountbatten of Burma* on 16 September 1980.

An unusual pairing at Bristol Temple Meads as No. 33028 (D6546) double heads an unidentified 'Peak' on a Travelling Post Office train. July 1986.

At Finchdean, just north of Havant, No. 33028 is powering along with a twelve-car train formed of 1963 EMU stock. Headcode 55 was not generally used on the south-western division and I've not been able to find the reason for the drag. There does look to be remnants of snow on the ground.

At Poole we find No. 33029 (D6547) in charge of a nuclear flask carrier, sandwiched between a pair of HEA hoppers used as barrier vehicles and a BR standard brake van. This was a working from Hamworthy to Eastleigh. 27 April 1987. (G. Roose)

Approaching Clapham Junction a scruffy-looking No. 33030 (D6548) heads south-west with the Venice Simplon Orient Express Pullman set, working a Bournemouth Belle charter. March 1988.

At Millbrook we find No. 33030 coasting towards Southampton whilst working 1O33, the 08.00 Cardiff Central to Portsmouth Harbour, although headcode 79 denotes a service to Portsmouth and Southsea. 7 March 1988. (P. Barber)

Near Blackwater we find No. 33030 and a smart set of Southern Region Mk1 coaches forming a 'Footex' football charter for Brighton & Hove Albion. They are away at Hereford. The train will run via the Reading Severn Tunnel and Maindee Junction to reach its destination. The result was 1-1, with Brighton taking the lead in 50 seconds and Peter Ward scoring on his first team debut. 27 March 1976.

Departing from Portsmouth and Southsea No. 33031 is working 1V66, the 13.10 Portsmouth Harbour to Bristol Temple Meads, once again with headcode 79 showing when it should be 89. First-class passengers are getting the relative comfort of a Mk2 vehicle. From the May 1988 timetable Class 155 Sprinters would start to take over services on this route. That didn't end well. 24 March 1988. (P. Barber)

Bromford Bridge in Birmingham finds Class 33 No. 6550 (later 33032) under the M6 viaduct. This area was the site of the Metro-Cammell railway works and not far from the Cromptons' birthplace in Smethwick. 1969.

Passing westbound through Chertsey, No. 33032 finds itself in charge of a train of empty flat wagons. July 1986.

Stormy skies loom overhead as No. 33033 (D6551) brakes for the station stop at Fareham whilst working 1O40, the 09.50 Swansea to Portsmouth Harbour. 26 March 1988. (P. Barber)

Formed of mainly first-class Mk2 stock, No. 33034 (D6552) works a race day special to Lingfield from Victoria, seen here at its destination. October 1978. (A. Edwards)

No. 33035 (D6553) approaches Warminster station whilst working 1V22, the 08.30 Brighton to Cardiff Central service. The five-car Mk1 coaching sets were typical for the route, but rarely were two formed the same. The locomotive was named *Spitfire* in 1994, having the plates transferred from No. 33047. 17 September 1985.

Clapham Yard finds No. D6554 (later 33036) along with No. D6511 (later 33101). This was the livery the Cromptons were delivered in. Some later gained small yellow warning panels and a few full yellow ends. The Southern Region was very slow with the yellow paint. 8 March 1964.

At Newton Abbot No. 33037 (D6555) accelerates away from the station stop whilst working 2C21, the 17.25 from Exeter St Davids to Paignton. 23 August 1985.

Passing under one of the multiple signal gantries at Kensington Olympia, No. 33038 (D6556) heads south with a very mixed bag of wagons. Included are some ferry vans, 21-ton coal hoppers and Presflo cement wagons. The headcode FG denoted a train from the Eastern Region to Norwood Junction. 28 October 1975.

Passing through East Croydon station is No. 33039 (D6557) with a short formation of Royal Train coaches, having earlier worked to Tattenham Corner for the Epsom Derby. 4 June 1980. (A. Edwards)

With Northiam cement terminal to the left and the River Itchen to the right No. 33040 (D6558) potters towards Southampton with a train of 35-ton type B tank wagons. In the distance a 3H DEMU and a Class 47 on a short container train can be seen. May 1979.

Class 33 No. 33042 (D6560) rests between duties at Clapham Junction. 1977.

With just four cement wagons in tow No. 33043 (D6561) is at Westbury. September 1986. (I. Whitmarsh)

Heading east at Goring by Sea No. 33044 (D6562) is working 1O33, the 09.05 Bristol Temple Meads to Brighton. July 1987.

At Southall Cromptons Nos 33045 (D6563) and 33040 make a fine sight as they double head a train of empty Amey Roadstone PGA hoppers returning to Westbury. 25 January 1980.

A very rare train just north of the Skew bridge between Merstham and Coulsdon. No. 33045 hurries northwards on the Quarry line with a train of loaded container flats. The 1K headcode suggests a train from Newhaven, which has had limited container traffic in the past. Image taken from Woodplace Lane bridge. April 1983. (A. Miles)

No. 33046 (D6564) accelerates away from the station stop at Westbury whilst working 1V38, the 09.10 Portsmouth Harbour to Cardiff Central service. In 1991 the locomotive was named *Merlin*. 12 March 1987. (P. Barber)

Rolling into Salisbury we find No. 33047 (D6565) working 1O73, the 11.10 Bristol Temple Meads to Portsmouth Harbour service. In 1991 the locomotive gained the nameplates *Spitfire*. 14 March 1985.

Passing through Eastleigh No. 33048 (D6566) has charge of a long train of car transporters. Cartic 4 wagons loaded with Ford Escorts sandwich carflats loaded with Transit vans. They look like Mk3 transits, which will date the image to 1986.

Curving off the Salisbury line at Redbridge is No. 33049 (D6567) working an unidentified Bristol Temple Meads to Portsmouth Harbour service. Passing it is No. 47083 *Orion* with a loaded Amey Roadstone aggregates train. 4 July 1984. (P. Barber)

Nearly at the end of its journey No. 33050 (D6568) runs into Exeter Central station whilst working 1V09, the 09.10 London Waterloo to Exeter St Davids. In 1988 the locomotive gained the name *Isle of Grain*. 2 April 1983.

Nos 33051 (D6569) and 33053 (D6571) arrive at Angmering to pick up passengers for an excursion to Great Yarmouth run by the West Sussex Railway Touring Trust, which started at Chichester. The Cromptons will work the train to Kensington Olympia where No. 47180 will take the train forward. No. 33051 gained the name *Shakespeare Cliff* in 1988. 27 August 1979. (J. Vaughan)

A rather deserted East Croydon station as No. 33052 (D6570) *Ashford* passes through with a train of UKF Fertiliser pallet vans en route from Horsham back to Ince and Elton near Ellesmere Port. April 1987.

Coulsdon North station and No. 33052 comes off the Redhill line with a train of oil tankers probably from the terminal at Salfords that served Gatwick Airport. It was named *Ashford* in 1980. 4 August 1979.

With snow on the ground No. 33053 (D6571) arrives at Honiton with 1V61, the 08.53 (SO) Brighton to Exeter St Davids service. 6 January 1979.

Apart from a couple of trainspotters Clapham Junction appears deserted as No. 33054 (D6572) pauses for a crew change. The PCA cement hoppers will be en route back to Northfleet cement works, now the home of the Bluewater shopping centre.

London Bridge low level finds No. 33055 (D6573) waiting to depart with 2U19, the 17.20 London Bridge to Uckfield service. This was the first of four loco-hauled evening peak departures to the Oxted line. The other three services ran to East Grinstead. A similar pattern ran to London Bridge in the mornings. 20 August 1979.

Heading south at Shortlands No. 33055 works a pair of nuclear flask wagons, which are sandwiched by a pair of former ferry vans. The ensemble is en route to Dungeness. August 1986.

No. 33056 (D6574) *The Burma Star* pauses at Westbury whilst working 1V46, the 08.30 Brighton to Cardiff Central service. The locomotive was named at Waterloo station on 1 September 1980. After No. 33056 was withdrawn from service the nameplates were transferred to No. 33202. 10 April 1987.

Below the spaghetti of overhead wires No. 33057 (D6575), with its train of tank wagons, joins the West Coast main line from the West London line at Willesden Junction. It was later named *Seagull* in 1991. October 1978.

Southern Region Locomotives in the 1970s and 1980s

At Shelwick in Herefordshire No. 33058 (D6577) leans into the curve with an unidentified Manchester Piccadilly to Cardiff Central service. 4 April 1985.

In rural Wiltshire at Great Wishford, between Wilton and Salisbury, No. 33059 (D6578) plods along with a lengthy train of loaded Grampus wagons heading for Basingstoke. 9 May 1985.

In bright autumn sunshine No. 33060 (D6579) approaches Salisbury with an engineers' train. 29 September 1987.

No. 33061 (D6581) is found stabled between duties at Reading as No. 33107 (D6520) sporting white cab surrounds passes by with a loaded Freightliner train. 15 February 1983. (B. Watkins)

Arriving at Reading we find No. 33062 (D6582) hauling a parcels train bound for Redhill. No. 47531 waits to pick up an Intercity service to or from Poole. 4 August 1977.

It's a misty day in North Kent as No. 33063 (D6583) comes off the Chatham line at Strood heading light engine towards Hoo Junction or Hither Green depot. 27 September 1985.

At Laira Junction, Plymouth, No. 33064 (D6584) along with No. 33042 run light engine. The locomotives had worked to Plymouth on a railtour from London Paddington, in connection with an open day at Laira depot. 15 September 1991.

Its New Year's Day and No. 33065 (D6585) heads an unidentified Bristol Temple Meads to Portsmouth Harbour service at Bathampton. A chocolate and cream Mk1 coach is a colourful interloper. A rake of these were repainted for a season of steam-worked services to Torbay. In 1991 it was named *Sealion*. 1 January 1986.

No. 33065 departs from Selhurst Yard with an engineers' train loaded with spoil. An unidentified sister locomotive watches proceedings. 10 March 1983. (A. Miles)

For the Bournemouth electrification nineteen Class 33s were fitted with buffing plates, buckeye couplings and high-level jumper cables to control the 4TC push-pull sets and other 1963 type stock. Classified 33/1, the first of the class, No. 33101 (D6511), is seen here at Gillingham (Dorset) with a 4TC set working a Salisbury to Waterloo stopping service. 13 August 1988.

Clearly showing off all the modifications to make this sub-class of push-pull fitted locomotives, No. 33102 (D6513) pauses at Basingstoke with a Salisbury to Waterloo service.

You would struggle to guess where this scene was as No. 33103 (D6514) lays down some clag, heading east with a trainload of 45-ton TTA tank wagons. It's approaching West Worthing station. (J. Vaughan)

Southern Region Locomotives in the 1970s and 1980s

Strong sunshine highlights No. 33104 (D6516) on the approaches to London Waterloo station. 11 April 1978. (P. Barber)

Looking smart with its white-painted cab surrounds No. 33105 (D6517) arrives at Southampton whilst working 1O13, the 08.21 Leeds to Weymouth cross-country service. 1 August 1983.

Worting Junction near Basingstoke finds No. 33106 (D6519) and a 4TC set working a Reading to Portsmouth Harbour service. Formed of DEMUs during the week, on Sundays the service was worked by Cromptons and 4TC sets. February 1988.

Departing from Poole, No. 33107 and a pair of 4TC sets forms 1W23, the 11.32 Waterloo to Weymouth service. The Crompton would take the train on at Bournemouth, it having been propelled from Waterloo by a 4REP unit. 3 February 1987. (I. J. Stewart)

A plume of exhaust trails No. 33108 (D6521) as it curves on the Portsmouth direct line at Havant with a parcels and mail train bound for London Waterloo. The route towards Chichester can be seen in the background. 21 July 1989. (J. Vaughan)

It's a nice sunny day as a grubby No. 33109 (D6525) starts 1W34, the 15.31 Weymouth to London Waterloo service away from Wareham station. On 3 July 1993 it gained the name *Captain Bill Smith RNR*. 27 August 1987.

Captured on the Weymouth tramway at Nicholas Street, No. 33110 (D6527) works its way slowly from the Quayside station back to Weymouth. 10 September 1984.

Nos 33111 (D6528) and 33009 slow for the junction at Basingstoke to take this Freightliner train towards Reading. A young trainspotter and father watch the proceedings. No. 33111 shows what years of going through the carriage washer does to the paint finish. 13 August 1983.

It's the summer months, although from the thick coats the ladies are wearing you'd think otherwise. No. 33112 (D6529) waits to depart from Weymouth Quay with a Channel Islands boat train for London Waterloo. The portable bell and flashing lamp for use on the tramway can clearly be seen on the secondman's side lamp bracket. The locomotive was named *Templecombe* in 1987. June 1984.

In 1984 prior to the introduction of the non-stop Gatwick Express service from London Victoria British Rail ran a series of travel agency promotional exhibitions. This went to many cities throughout the country. At Holgate Bridge, York, we find No. 33113 (D6531), plus Gatwick Express sets 8306 and 8201 and (out of view) Mk1 BCK S21273. 1984.

1O19, the 07.52 Newcastle to Poole, gets underway from Reading after a locomotive change. No. 33114 (D6532) provides power for the trip through to the destination. No. 33114 had the *Sultan* nameplates transferred to it in 1988, then carried *Ashford 150* nameplates for a short period in 1992/3. 25 February 1981.

The end of the line is Weymouth Quay and No. D6533 (later 33115) has just arrived with a Channel Islands boat train from Waterloo, formed of 4TC sets. 1973.

No. 33116 (D6538) accelerates away from Reading with 1O13, the 07.00 Newcastle to Poole, whilst a Class 47/0 has just been attached to 1E63, the 11.39 from Poole going forward to Sheffield with portions for Newcastle and Leeds. It was named *Hertfordshire Railtours* in December 1993. April 1974.

Unusually berthed in the north-east bay platforms at Kensington Olympia is No. 33116 and 4TC set 403. These combinations regularly ran the Clapham Junction to Kensington Olympia peak-time service. Known as the 'Kenny Belle', the trains have had various stock over the years from a couple of coaches and locomotive to DEMUs and DMUs. In the distance the huge Charles House complex is silhouetted against the West London skyline. 1 March 1979.

An interesting low shot of Nos 33117 (D6536) and 33109 at Southampton Central waiting to depart with a parcels train. 20 July 1985. (R. Marsh)

On the West London line near West Brompton we find No. 33118 (D6538) and a 4TC set forming 2Y84, the 17.15 'Kenny Belle' peak-only shuttle between Clapham Junction and Kensington Olympia. 14 April 1989.

At London Paddington we find No. 33119 towing 4TC set 420 towards Reading. It is a Sunday so I'm guessing this is an engineering work alteration, with the Bournemouth main line blocked somewhere. 25 June 1978. (G. Roose)

The Saturdays-only Brighton to the West Country service was formed of coaching stock from Clapham Yard and locomotives more often than not from Hither Green depot. On this grey summer's day we find a pair of Hastings line Cromptons, Nos 33201 (D6586) and 33211 (D6596), heading 1V10, the 09.13 Brighton to Penzance, at Millbrook, Southampton. 7 June 1986.

Eleven Class 33s were built to the narrower loading gauge on the Hastings line. The loading gauge was narrower due to various tunnels having to be strengthened as they were not built to specification to save the builders money. Second in class, No. 33202 (D6587) is captured powering through Chislehurst with a long train of European wagons heading for the train ferry at Dover. March 1987.

Powering through the Down fast line at Tonbridge is No. 33203 (D6588) with an unidentified passenger train. It could be a Merrymaker excursion or possibly the SAGA holiday train to Margate.

A wet and windy looking Southampton Central as Nos 33204 (D6589) and 33063 pause whilst working 1V10, the 09.13 Saturdays-only Brighton to Penzance. The driver looks back for the tip to depart. 13 September 1986.

Just over six months later than the previous photo and a much smarter-looking No. 33204 has just arrived with a 4TC from Basingstoke. The locomotive will run round the train and work back to Basingstoke as 2Z02 at 17.24. The locomotive was also noted on a later Waterloo to Salisbury service. There must have been a shortage of Class 33/1s for this unusual formation. 3H DEMU No. 205032 (1132) can be seen in the adjacent platform. 17 April 1987.

Running into Portsmouth & Southsea low level station is No. 33205 (D6590) with an unidentified service from Bristol Temple Meads. March 1988. (J. Skinner)

Stratford-upon-Avon is the unlikely location to find 'Slim Jim' No. 33206 (D6591). The loco had arrived there on a VSOE charter from London. A Class 122 DMU can be seen in the adjacent platform. 28 June 1984.

A clean No. 33207 (D6592) gets away from Bristol Temple Meads with an unidentified working. This had the *Earl Mountbatten of Burma* nameplates transferred to it when No. 33027 was withdrawn. 17 May 1982.

At Crewe No. 87009 *City of Birmingham* appears to have been assisting a poorly No. 33208 (D6593). The Crompton is presumably on a Cardiff to Crewe working.

Very slick working was required at London Bridge to operate the Oxted line loco-hauled services. The previous inbound locomotive was used to take the next train out. Here we find No. D6594 (later 33209) arriving with an ECS train from New Cross Gate. 3 August 1972.

Being sent to Coventry is where we find No. 33209 and on frontline Intercity duties too. Pressed into service due to the failure of No. 47652 at Poole, No. 33209 has reached the West Midlands working 1M23, the 15.08 Poole to Manchester Piccadilly. 11 July 1988.

Lydd in Kent is where we find No. 33210 (D6595), with No. 33212 (D6597) at the other end of the train. The occasion is the F&W railtour 'Darkle Dungeneer'. The railtour had originated at Plymouth and had traction from Classes 47 and 56, as well as the Cromptons. 28 July 1985.

Crossing the River Avon at Bradford-upon-Avon, No. 33211 (D6596) is reflected in the still waters whilst working 1V54, the 10.10 Portsmouth Harbour to Swansea. This is the penultimate day of Class 33 workings on this route as Class 155 Sprinters take over from 16 May. 14 May 1988. (G. Roose)

At Etchingham we find 'Slim Jim' No. 33212 heading south from Northfleet cement works with a trainload of hoppers heading to British Gypsum at Mountfield. 29 May 1985.

Although never renumbered as such, the three Southern 'Booster' locomotives were allocated Class 70. A very misty Hastings is the location for No. 20001 (CC1) as it runs round its train. This is the 'Sussex Venturer' railtour operated by the Locomotive Club of Great Britain. The trip originated at London Waterloo and included various routes in London before heading to the coast. The passengers will be glad that the steam heating boiler is working well. 4 January 1969.

No. 20001 (CC1) is found stabled at Stewarts Lane depot. The three locomotives mainly stayed on the central division working freight trains, as well as the London Victoria to Newhaven boat trains. All three could run off the third rail or using the pantograph in the few yards equipped with trolley wires. CC1 and CC2 looked very similar but CC3 had very different cab ends. 1961.

Introduced in early 1959, the Class 71s were a development of the earlier Class 70 but in a much smaller body. At Ashford (Kent) we find No. E5001 (later 71001) pausing with a parcels train. A member of traincrew looks back down the train, awaiting the tip to depart. 21 August 1973.

The Class 71s didn't have a long life; many were stored by 1976 and withdrawn shortly after. At Hither Green depot Nos 71004 (E5004) and 71009 (E5009) await their fate. March 1977.

No. 71010 (E5010) heads north through Ashford (Kent) with the Dover Western Docks to London Bridge TPO (Travelling Post Office). 14 July 1975.

Eighteen months after withdrawal No. 71014 (E5014) and a sister locomotive slowly rust away at Hither Green depot. It won't be until September before it gets cut up. 31 March 1979.

The Class 73 locomotives have been probably British Railways' most versatile build. The Class 73/0 locomotives are easily recognised by the two small grills on the body side and the additional jumper cable not present on the Class 73/1s. At Eastleigh we find No. 73001 with a van train bound for London Waterloo. The first six were classified class 'JA' and the main batch 'JB' by the Southern Region. 1979.

A lone trainspotter sits amongst the detritus on the end of platform 11 at Clapham Junction as No. E6002 (later 73002) shunts parcels stock into Clapham Yard. 1972.

Four of the Class 73/0s were transferred to Merseyrail after the privatisation of British Rail. They were used for engineering and Sandite duties. At Hall Road depot we find No. 73002 with No. 73001 in the rear. 3 July 1994.

Stewarts Lane is the location for this image of No. 73003 (E6003). Later named *Sir Herbert Walker*, it is preserved at the Swindon & Cricklade Railway.

In Redhill sidings No. 73004 (E6004) is stabled alongside a Class 119 Gloucester cross-country DMU. This locomotive was later named *The Bluebell Railway*. 22 July 1979. (K. Oxlade)

In a very rural setting near Goring-by-Sea No. 73004 powers along the West Coastway route with 1V12, the 09.05 SO Brighton to Plymouth service. By this date the train ran via Portsmouth where a Class 50 or 47 would take the train forward. 1989. (J. Vaughan)

Passing the now closed Coulsdon North station No. E6005 (later 73005) powers south with a London Bridge to Littlehampton van train. Bar the leading former Southern PMV van the rest of train is formed of BR CCT vans. 2 April 1970.

Making a change from parcels and freight train duties No. 73005 passes Hook with 1W91, the 09.54 Waterloo to Weymouth Quay, Channel Islands boat train. 10 October 1980.

Shunting Grampus wagons at Redhill is No. 73006 (E6006). In the background are some hopper wagons loaded with sand from Holmthorpe. 13 October 1984. (J. Vaughan)

With the second man leaning out of the window to hand the token to the signalman, No. 73101 (E6007) curves off the branch line from Lavant heading to Drayton with gravel. This was a very short freight working from one side of Chichester to the other using these French-built side discharge wagons. No. 73101 was later named *Brighton Evening Argus* and then renamed *The Royal Alex* after the Brighton children's hospital. July 1974.

No. E6008 (later 73102, 73212) powers through Lancing with the Chichester/Littlehampton to London van train. This service conveyed mainly salad items from various Sussex market gardens. The locomotive was later named *Airtour Suisse*. 1971.

Running light engine towards Eastleigh, No. 73103 (E6009) is captured at St Denys. 6 July 1987. (P. Barber)

A nice night shot at Southampton of Nos 73104 (E6010) and 73130 (E6037) working 1B46, the 18.47 SuO Poole to Waterloo service. When the Class 442 EMUs were being built for the Weymouth electrification pairs of Class 73s substituted for the 4REP units as these were withdrawn and the traction motors reused in the new trains. The Southern Region wasted nothing if it could avoid it. 22 January 1989. (P. Barber)

With strong sunlight filtering through the station roof, No. 73105 (E6011) is looking smart in Large Logo livery. The locomotive is at Brighton having worked a Gatwick Express test train. March 1984. (A.Gibbs)

No. E6012 (later 73106) is seen here at Brighton having arrived with a van train from Bricklayers Arms.

Nos 73107 (E6013) and 73212 (E6008, 73102) pass through Farnborough on a Weymouth to Waterloo service. A former 4REP buffet car has been added to one of the 4TC sets. 21 September 1988. (J. Vaughan)

Passing through Cuxton is No. 73108 (E6014) working a train of empty Marinex sea dredged gravel wagons from Salfords back to Cliffe for reloading. 28 June 1984.

A pristine No. 73109 (E6015) pilots No. 33025 *Sultan* out of Clapham Junction carriage sidings towards Waterloo. No. 73109 was later named *Battle of Britain 50th anniversary*. 2 October 1986. (P. Barber)

No. 73110 (E6016) pauses at Basingstoke with a long train of Mk2 Ford Transits being delivered from the factory at Eastleigh. Not surprisingly, white seems to be the most popular colour. 1 June 1982.

From 1984 until the early 2000s the Gatwick Express service was the mainstay of workings for the Class 73/1s. At Salfords heading to Gatwick we find No. 73111 (E6017) with the standard winter months five-car formation plus luggage van. 14 April 1986. (P. Barber)

No. 73112 (E6018, later 73213) is at East Croydon to assist with the recovery of two trains involved in an earlier collision. See the caption for No. 73115 for more details. It was named *University of Kent at Canterbury* in 1990. 16 January 1982. (J. Vaughan)

In the yard at East Wimbledon depot we find No. 73113 (E6019, later 73211) moving coaches from one of the 4PEP and the 2PEP prototype suburban units. Experience gained from these units went into Classes 507, 508 and 313, etc. It was named *County of West Sussex* in 1986. 16 December 1976. (C. J. Marsden)

Running light engine out of Lovers Walk depot into Brighton station is No. 73114 (E6020). It gained the name *Stewarts Lane TMD* in 1994. August 1979.

No. 73115 (E6021) was involved in a big collision at East Croydon. Working an engineers train from Three Bridges to New Cross Gate, it passed a signal at danger and hit the rear of a Brighton to London Bridge parcels train already occupying platform one. Here some of the resulting damage can be seen, with a Mk1 GUV nearly on its side in the former yard. The damage was so severe the locomotive was withdrawn and scrapped. 16 January 1982. (A. Edwards)

With some empty stock for Waterloo No. 73116 (E6022, later 73210) waits to depart. It was named *Selhurst* in 1986. 30 August 1983.

Arriving at Gatwick Airport with 1D10, the 11.15 from London Victoria, is No. 73117 (E6023). The train has run via Redhill, headcode 30. The usual route via the Quarry line was headcode 20. This locomotive was also named *University of Surrey* in 1987. 27 June 1985.

Dropping down towards Longhedge Junction at Clapham No. 73118 (E6024) is working an empty aggregates train, probably back to Cliffe in Kent. This was one of the locomotives later fitted with coupling adaptors to work with the Class 373 Eurostar trains. It was also later named *The Romney, Hythe and Dymchurch Railway*. 10 March 1983.

With a former London Midland inspection saloon No. 73119 (E6025) *Kentish Mercury* propels the consist through Clapham Junction on the Windsor lines.

In a barren scene No. 73120 (E6026, later 73209) has charge of the Chipmans weedkilling train. After some head scratching and some help from the guys on RMweb, we believe that the location is the former Feltham Marshalling Yard. This location is being reactivated as sidings for South West Trains new Class 701 units. Some may even be in service by the time this is published. 3 May 1976. (C. J. Marsden)

Southampton Eastern Docks and we find No. 73121 (E6028, later 73208) being escorted through the traffic. It looks like a Volvo Amazon and Peugeot 104 are held up. This was another named locomotive gaining plates in 1983 for *Croydon 1883–1983*. (C. J. Marsden)

Brighton station and No. 73122 (E6029, later 73207) *County of East Sussex* has just arrived with the Royal Train, with Elizabeth II visiting Brighton. 16 July 1985. (A. Gibbs)

No. 73123 (E6030, later 73206) *Gatwick Express*, along with a sister locomotive, is in Stewarts Lane depot. April 1985.

Woking finds No. 73124 (E6031, later 73205) working a Channel Islands boat train whilst Crompton No. 33033 can be seen the adjacent platform. It was named *London Chamber of Commerce* in 1987. 19 May 1982. (M. McDermott)

Not the most scenic of railway locations but Hoo Junction is where we find No. 73125 (E6032, later 73204). This was named *Stewarts Lane* in 1985. 11 September 1981.

On a lovely summer's day we find a grubby No. 73126 (E6033) powering through Clapham Junction with a Channel Islands boat train. Looks like a West of England Mk2 coaching set has been used, complete with TSOT micro-buffet. Another locomotive that gained nameplates, it became *Kent & East Sussex Railway* in 1991. 14 June 1981.

A shortage of EMU stock led to a Brighton to London Bridge return peak time working revert to locomotive haulage. At Forest Hill we find No. 73127 (E6034, later 73203) heading south with 1G69, the 17.55 London Bridge to Brighton. 23 May 1979.

No. 73128 (E6035) propels a Gatwick Express service through East Croydon, en route to London Victoria. The number 7 on the lamp bracket denoted the circuit number. Seven sets were usually used, although it could be run with just five but with some very tight turnarounds at each terminus. This gained the name *OVS Bulleid CBE* in 1991. June 1984.

Strong autumn sunlight illuminates No. 73129 (E6036) *City of Winchester*, which looks very smart whilst working 1D34, the 14.15 London Victoria to Gatwick Airport service, seen here approaching East Croydon. 27 October 1984.

Under the overhead lines at Willesden Junction No. 73130 (E6037) slows to a halt with a long train of ferry vans from Dover and an engineers' Weltrol wagon leading the consist. *City of Portsmouth* nameplates were applied in 1988. October 1978.

Definitely not displaying the correct headcode, No. 73131 rushes through Wandsworth Common with a Gatwick Express service. It was named *County of Surrey* in 1988. June 1984.

Curving and climbing up from the Great Western Main Line at Old Oak Common is No. 73131 (E6038). It will shortly join the West London line at North Pole Junction before heading south over the Thames with its load of house coal bound for Chessington South. 29 October 1981.

No. 73132 (E6039) makes light of this engineers' train at Salfords (Surrey), almost certainly bound for Three Bridges Yard.

No. 73133 (E6040) is berthed in Chichester Yard along with a motley collection of wagons including some engineers' wagons, a couple of 12-ton vans and a ferry tank wagon. This gained the nameplates transferred from No. 73004 and is preserved on the Bluebell Railway. 17 March 1983. (J. Vaughan)

No. 73134 (E6041) provides the motive power for 4B22, the 12.23 Brighton to London Bridge vans. An unidentified but named Class 47 has brought the stock into the platform. This locomotive was named *Woking Homes 1885–1985* in 1985. 29 September 1988. (J. Vaughan)

Stormy skies threaten at Farnborough as No. 73135 (E6042, later 73235) on an empty van train overtakes No. 73112 with a coal train. 1 November 1977.

At Hither Green depot we find No. 73136 (E6043) *Kent Youth Music* in the later version of the Network SouthEast livery. Behind it is sister locomotive No. 73105 in the rather plain grey livery. 28 May 1995.

At Southampton we find No. 73137 (E6044) on an unidentified service bound for Waterloo alongside 3H DEMU No. 1127 on a Salisbury to Portsmouth Harbour stopping service. No. 73137 was named *Royal Observer Corps* in 1985. 11 August 1983. (J. Binnie)

A misty Beeding cement works on the stump of line that originally ran from Shoreham-by-Sea to Christs Hospital is where we find No. E6045 (later 73138). The cement works Ruston and Hornsby diesel mechanical shunter can been seen. July 1969.

Running under Clapham Junction 'A' signal box is No. 73139 (E6046) with an ECS working from London Waterloo. An unidentified Class 50 is still attached at the rear.

It's a grim day at Beckenham Junction as No. 73140 (E6047) shunts its coal train into the Coal Concentration Depot. The Southern Region south-eastern divisional HQ was at Beckenham along with the regional ticket office training school. March 1979.

Heading towards Lavant with the empty gravel hoppers from Drayton is No. 73141 (E6048). The Francis Parker company dug out the gravel at Lavant. It ran via a conveyor belt to be loaded into the hoppers. The train then ran to the east side of Chichester at Drayton and were discharged into pits to be washed. 18 August 1990.

Taken from a multistorey car park at East Croydon, ex-works No. 73142 (E6049, later 73201) takes the Royal Train south from Victoria to Tattenham Corner for the Derby Day meeting at the racecourse. Later that year it was named *Broadlands* and was the favoured locomotive for Royal Train duties and VIP specials. 4 June 1980. (A. Edwards)

The perceived need for more electro-diesel locomotives and the loss of traffic for the Class 71 saw ten former Class 71s rebuilt as Class 74s. Paxman diesel engines were installed, but they were not a successful class and barely lasted ten years. Apart from some cross-London freight workings they barely strayed from the south-western division. No. E6103 (E5006, later 74003) is seen here at Southampton propelling a pair of 4TC sets.

At London Waterloo we find No. E6105 (E5019, later 74005) on the stops, having recently arrived with a train from the ocean liner terminal at Southampton. 6 July 1972.

At Eastleigh Yard we find No. E6106 (E5023, later 74006) berthed alongside a newly delivered 4VEP for the Bournemouth line electrification.

Curving through platform 9 at Clapham Junction is No. 74008 (E5005, E6108) whilst working 1W91, the 09.36 Waterloo to Weymouth Quay Channel Island boat train. 28 September 1977.